the ROSARY

THE GREAT WEAPON OF THE 21ST CENTURY

A GUIDE TO PRAYING THE ROSARY

To order more copies of this booklet
if you live in the **United States**, contact:

America Needs Fatima
(888) 317-5571
P.O. Box 341, Hanover, PA 17331
www.ANF.org · ANF@ANF.org

To order more copies of this booklet
if you live in **Canada**, contact:

Canada Needs Our Lady
1-844-729-6279 or (844-Say-Mary)
P.O. Box 36040, Greenfield Park, QC J4V 3N7
www.CanadaNeedsOurLady.org

How to PRAY the ROSARY

1. Make the Sign of the Cross and say the Apostles Creed.
2. Say the Our Father.
3. Say three Hail Marys.
4. Say the Glory Be. Announce the first Mystery and say the Our Father.
5. Say ten Hail Marys while meditating on the Mystery.
6. Say the Glory Be. Say the Fatima prayers. Announce the second Mystery and say the Our Father.
7. Say ten Hail Marys while meditating on the Mystery.
8. Say the Glory Be. Say the Fatima prayers. Announce the third Mystery and say the Our Father.
9. Say ten Hail Marys while meditating on the Mystery.
10. Say the Glory Be. Say the Fatima prayers. Announce the fourth Mystery and say the Our Father.
11. Say ten Hail Marys while meditating on the Mystery.
12. Say the Glory Be. Say the Fatima prayers. Announce the fifth Mystery and say the Our Father.
13. Say ten Hail Marys while meditating on the Mystery.
14. Say the Glory Be. Say the Fatima prayers. Say the Hail Holy Queen and the prayer to St. Michael the Archangel.

"**P**ray the rosary every day to obtain peace for the world and the end of the war," Our Lady said to the three young shepherds of Fatima on May 13, 1917. In each of the six apparitions, she insisted on the necessity of the daily rosary.

When praying the rosary it is important to remember to meditate on the life of Our Lord. Each decade or mystery corresponds to an episode in the life of Our Lord Jesus Christ or of the Blessed Virgin Mary.

When praying the Hail Mary it is important to pronounce the Holy Name of Jesus with great reverence. This means that when the rosary is being prayed in a group, before joining in with the second part of the Hail Mary, those answering the prayers should wait until after whoever is leading has finished the first part. Otherwise the Holy Name of Jesus will not be uttered and meditated upon with due reverence.

At Fatima, Our Lady requested that we pray one rosary of five decades every day. It is good and praiseworthy to pray more than one rosary each day if and when possible.

PRAYERS

The Sign of the Cross
In the name of the Father, and of the Son, and of the Holy Ghost. Amen.

The Apostles' Creed
I believe in God, the Father Almighty, Creator of Heaven and earth, and in Jesus Christ, His only Son, Our Lord, Who was conceived by the Holy Ghost,

born of the Virgin Mary, suffered under Pontius Pilate, was crucified, died, and was buried. He descended into Hell; the third day He rose again from the dead; He ascended into Heaven, and sitteth at the right hand of God, the Father Almighty; from thence He shall come to judge the living and the dead. I believe in the Holy Ghost, the Holy Catholic Church, the communion of saints, the forgiveness of sins, the resurrection of the body, and life everlasting. Amen.

The Our Father
Our Father, Who art in Heaven, hallowed be Thy name; Thy kingdom come, Thy will be done on earth as it is in Heaven. Give us this day our daily bread, and forgive us our trespasses, as we forgive those who trespass against us, and lead us not into temptation, but deliver us from evil. Amen.

The Hail Mary
Hail, Mary, full of grace, the Lord is with thee. Blessed art thou among women, and blessed is the fruit of thy womb, Jesus. Holy Mary, Mother of God, pray for us sinners, now and at the hour of our death. Amen.

The Glory Be
Glory be to the Father, and to the Son, and to the Holy Ghost, as it was in the beginning, is now, and ever shall be, world without end. Amen.

The O My Jesus
O my Jesus, forgive us our sins, save us from the fires of hell, lead all souls to Heaven, especially those in most need of Thy mercy.

The Hail Holy Queen
Hail Holy Queen, Mother of Mercy, our life, our sweetness and our hope! To thee do we cry, poor banished children of Eve. To thee do we send up our sighs,

mourning and weeping in this valley of tears. Turn then, most gracious advocate, thine eyes of mercy towards us, and after this our exile, show unto us the blessed fruit of thy womb, Jesus. O clement, O loving, O sweet Virgin Mary.

V. Pray for us, O holy Mother of God.

R. That we may be made worthy of the promises of Christ.

Let us pray. O God, Whose only-begotten Son, by His life, death, and resurrection, has purchased for us the rewards of eternal life; grant, we beseech Thee, that meditating upon these mysteries of the most holy rosary of the Blessed Virgin Mary, we may imitate what they contain and obtain what they promise. Through the same Christ Our Lord. Amen..

Sub Tuum Praesidium
We fly to thy patronage, O holy Mother of God; despise not our petitons in our necessities, but deliver us from all dangers, O glorious and Blessed Virgin.

The Litany of the Blessed Virgin Mary
Lord, have mercy on us.
Christ, have mercy on us.
Lord, have mercy on us. Christ, hear us.
Christ, graciously hear us.
God the Father of heaven, *have mercy on us.*
God the Son, Redeemer of the world, *have mercy on us.*
God the Holy Ghost, *have mercy on us.*
Holy Trinity, one God, *have mercy on us.*
Holy Mary, *pray for us.*
(repeat *'pray for us'* after each invocation.)
Holy Mother of God,
Holy Virgin of virgins,
Mother of Christ,
Mother of divine grace,
Mother most pure,

Mother most chaste,
Mother inviolate,
Mother undefiled,
Mother most amiable,
Mother most admirable,
Mother of good counsel,
Mother of our Creator,
Mother of our Savior,
Virgin most prudent,
Virgin most venerable,
Virgin most renowned,
Virgin most powerful,
Virgin most merciful,
Virgin most faithful,
Mirror of justice,
Seat of wisdom,
Cause of our joy,
Spiritual vessel,
Vessel of honor,
Singular vessel of devotion,
Mystical rose,
Tower of David,
Tower of ivory,
House of gold,
Ark of the covenant,
Gate of heaven,
Morning star,
Health of the sick,
Refuge of sinners,
Comforter of the afflicted,
Help of Christians,
Queen of angels,
Queen of patriarchs,
Queen of prophets,
Queen of apostles,
Queen of martyrs,

Queen of confessors,
Queen of virgins,
Queen of all saints,
Queen conceived without original sin,
Queen assumed into heaven,
Queen of the most Holy Rosary,
Queen of families,
Queen of peace,

V. Lamb of God, Who takest away the sins of the world,

R. Spare us, O Lord.

V. Lamb of God, Who takest away the sins of the world,

R. Graciously hear us, O Lord.

V. Lamb of God, Who takest away the sins of the world,

R. Have mercy on us.

V. Pray for us, O Holy Mother of God.

R. That we may be made worthy of the promises of Christ.

Let us pray. Grant unto us, Thy servants, we beseech Thee, O Lord God, at all times to enjoy health of soul and body; and by the glorious intercession of Blessed Mary, ever virgin, when freed from the sorrows of this present life, to enter into that joy which hath no end. Through Christ Our Lord. Amen.

The Memorare

Remember, O most gracious Virgin Mary, that never was it known that anyone who fled to thy protection, implored thy help, or sought thy intercession, was left unaided. Inspired by this confidence, I fly unto thee, O Virgin of virgins, my Mother! To thee do I come, before thee I stand, sinful and sorrowful. O Mother of the Word Incarnate, despise not my petitions, but in thy mercy, hear and answer me. Amen.

The Magnificat

My soul doth magnify the Lord, and my spirit hath rejoiced in God my Savior.

Because He hath regarded the humility of His handmaid.

For behold, from henceforth all generations shall call me blessed.

Because He that is mighty hath done great things to me, and holy is His Name.

And His mercy is from generation unto generations, to them that fear Him.

He hath shewed might in his arm.

He hath scattered the proud in the conceit of their heart.

He hath put down the mighty from their seat, and hath exalted the humble.

He hath filled the hungry with good things, and the rich He hath sent empty away.

He hath received Israel His servant, being mindful of His mercy.

As He spoke to our fathers, to Abraham and to his seed for ever.

Glory be to the Father, and to the Son, and to the Holy Ghost, as it was in the beginning, is now, and ever shall be, world without end. Amen.

MEDITATION
on the ROSARY

*Saint Louis de Montfort's Summary
of the Life, Death and Glory
of Jesus and Mary in the Holy Rosary*

Creed
1. Faith in the presence of God.
2. Faith in the Gospel.
3. Faith in and obedience to the Pope as the Vicar of Jesus Christ.

Our Father
The unity of the one, true and living God.

First Hail Mary
In honor of the Eternal Father, Who begets the Son in contemplating Himself.

Second Hail Mary
In honor of the Eternal Word, Who is equal to the Father, with Whom He produces the Holy Ghost.

Third Hail Mary
In honor of the Holy Ghost, Who proceeds from the Father and the Son by way of love.

FIRST JOYFUL MYSTERY
The ANNUNCIATION

"Behold the handmaid of the Lord."

In this mystery we contemplate the Virgin Mary being greeted by the angel, who announces that she is to conceive and give birth to Christ, our Redeemer.

Let us ask the Virgin of virgins, by the holy joy that filled her Immaculate Heart, to drive from our souls the discouragement and harmful sadness caused by the difficulties of daily life in this our neopagan world.

Our Father: God's immense charity.

Hail Mary:

1. The unfortunate state of disobedient Adam, his just condemnation, and that of all his children.
2. The desires of the Patriarchs and Prophets who asked for the Messias.
3. The wishes and prayers of the Most Holy Virgin, which hastened the coming of the Messias, and her marriage to Saint Joseph.
4. The charity of the Eternal Father, Who gave us His Son.
5. The love of the Son, Who gave Himself for us.
6. The Archangel Gabriel's mission and salutation.
7. Mary's virginal fear.
8. The Most Holy Virgin's faith and consent.
9. The creation of the soul and the formation of the body of Jesus Christ in the womb of Mary by the Holy Ghost.
10. The angels' adoration of the Incarnate Word in the womb of Mary.

SECOND JOYFUL MYSTERY
The VISITATION

*"Blessed art thou among women, and
blessed is the fruit of thy womb."*
Luke 1:42

In this mystery we contemplate the Mother of the Creator going to visit her cousin Saint Elizabeth, whose son, John the Baptist, trembled with joy in the womb upon hearing the voice of Mary.

Let us ask the Mother of Good Counsel that we too may tremble with joy and devotion when the call of grace makes itself heard in the interior of our souls.

Our Father: God's adorable majesty.

Hail Mary:

1. The joy of the Heart of Mary, and the dwelling of the Incarnate Word in her womb for nine months.
2. The sacrifice Jesus Christ made of Himself to the Father on entering this world.
3. The delights of Jesus in the humble and virginal womb of Mary, and those of Mary in the possession of her God.
4. Saint Joseph's doubt concerning Mary's maternity.
5. The election of the chosen ones, decided between Jesus and Mary in her womb.
6. The fervor of Mary in her visit to Saint Elizabeth.
7. The salutation of Mary and the sanctification of Saint John the Baptist and his mother, Saint Elizabeth.
8. The Most Holy Virgin's gratitude toward God in the Magnificat.
9. Her charity and humility in serving her cousin.
10. The mutual dependence of Jesus and Mary and the dependence we should have on each of them.

THIRD JOYFUL MYSTERY
The NATIVITY

In this mystery we contemplate Our God, born of the Virgin Mary in Bethlehem, and laid in a manger because there was no room in the inn.

Let us ask Jesus, Mary and Joseph to give us the piety, serenity and fortitude that emanate from the holy grotto of Bethlehem.

Our Father: God's inexhaustible riches.

Hail Mary:
1. The scorn and rejection Mary and Joseph endured in Bethlehem.
2. The poverty of the stable wherein God came to the world.
3. Mary's high contemplation and surpassing love at the moment of Our Lord's birth.
4. The Eternal Word's departure from the womb of Mary while maintaining her virginity.
5. The angels' adoration and hymnody at the birth of Jesus Christ.
6. The captivating beauty of His divine infancy.
7. The coming of the shepherds to the stable with their small presents.
8. The circumcision of Jesus Christ, and His affectionate pains.
9. The imposition of the Name of Jesus, and its grandeur.
10. The adoration of the Magi Kings, and their gifts.

FOURTH JOYFUL MYSTERY
The PRESENTATION

"And thy own soul a sword shall pierce, that out of many hearts, thoughts may be revealed."
Luke 2:35

In this mystery we contemplate the Virgin Mary carrying her Son to Jerusalem to present Him to the Lord in accordance with the Law of Moses. In the Temple, she meets the old Simeon, who takes the Christ Child in his arms and prophesies that He will be the light to the gentiles, the glory of Israel, the rock of scandal for the perdition and salvation of many.

Let us ask the Most Holy Virgin for a fearless soul ablaze with love for Holy Mother Church, so that we also may be a light to our brethren and, if need be, a rock of scandal to our social circles.

Our Father: God's eternal wisdom.

Hail Mary:
1. Jesus and Mary's obedience to the Law.
2. Jesus' sacrifice of His humanity in the Temple.
3. Mary's sacrifice of her honor.
4. The joy and praise of Simeon and Anna the Prophetess.
5. The ransom of Jesus by the offering of two turtle doves.
6. The slaughter of the Holy Innocents by Herod in his cruelty.
7. The flight of Jesus into Egypt through Saint Joseph's obedience to the voice of the angel.
8. His mysterious stay in Egypt.
9. His return to Nazareth.
10. His growth in age and wisdom.

FIFTH JOYFUL MYSTERY
The FINDING *in the* TEMPLE

"Son, why hast thou done so to us?"
Luke 2:48

In this mystery we contemplate how the Virgin Mary, having lost her Son, found Him in the Temple after three days of wearisome search, listening to the Doctors of the Law and asking them questions.

Let us ask Mary Most Holy, by the merits of the anguish she suffered during her searching, to grant us an ever-increasing fidelity to the Church amidst the multiple perplexities that a faithful Catholic must undergo in our days.

Our Father: God's unfathomable sanctity.

Hail Mary:
1. Our Lord's hidden, laborious and obedient life in the house of Nazareth.
2. His preaching and finding in the Temple among the doctors.
3. His baptism by Saint John the Baptist.
4. His fasting and temptations in the desert.
5. His admirable preaching.
6. His astonishing miracles.
7. The selection of His twelve Apostles and the powers He gave them.
8. His marvellous transfiguration.
9. The washing of His Apostles' feet.
10. The institution of the Holy Eucharist.

FIRST SORROWFUL MYSTERY
The AGONY in the GARDEN

"Father, if Thou wilt, remove this chalice from Me: but yet not My Will, but Thine be done."
Luke 22:42

In this mystery we contemplate our Divine Redeemer praying in the Garden of Olives and sweating blood as He foresees the Passion He is to suffer. His apostles sleep.

Let us ask our dauntless Mother to remove from our souls all the cowardly optimism that invites us to sleep when we should be watching and praying, and to give us the virtue of seriousness so that we will courageously embrace suffering every time it comes our way.

Our Father: God's essential felicity.

Hail Mary:
1. The divine seclusions of Jesus Christ during His life, and especially His seclusion in the Garden of Olives.
2. His humble and fervent prayers during His life and on the eve of the Passion.
3. The patience and sweetness with which He bore His Apostles during His life and particularly in the Garden of Olives.
4. His soul's anxiety throughout His life and principally in the Garden of Olives.
5. The rivers of blood that sorrow caused to gush from His adorable being.
6. The consolation He willingly accepted from an angel during His agony.
7. His conformity to the will of His Father despite the aversion of His nature.
8. The valor with which He went to meet His executioners, and the force of the word with which He threw them to the ground and then raised them.
9. His betrayal by Judas and His arrest by the Jews.
10. His apostles' abandonment.

SECOND SORROWFUL MYSTERY
The SCOURGING
at the PILLAR

"Thou shouldst not have any power against Me, unless it were given thee from above"

In this mystery we contemplate Our Lord Jesus Christ bound to the pillar and mercilessly flogged at the order of Pilate, who wanted to please the crowd.

Let us ask the Mother of Divine Grace to give us, whenever we are beset by tribulation, the strength and perseverance shown by her Son as the blows of the lash tore into His undefiled flesh for our sins.

Our Father: God's admirable patience.

Hail Mary:
1. The chains and ropes that bound Jesus.
2. The blow He received in the house of Caiphas.
3. The denials of Saint Peter.
4. The ignominies He suffered in the house of Herod when the white robe was put on Him.
5. The removal of all His garments.
6. The scorn and insults He suffered from His executioners because of His nakedness.
7. The thorny rods and the cruel whips with which they beat and tore Him.
8. The pillar to which He was tied.
9. The blood He shed and the wounds He received.
10. His fall in His own blood out of weakness..

THIRD SORROWFUL MYSTERY
The CROWNING
with THORNS

"Art Thou a king then?"
John 18:37

In this mystery we contemplate the King of Kings despoiled of His garments and clothed in a scarlet cloak. He is crowned with thorns, crushed with blows, overwhelmed with affronts and outrages by the procurator's brutal soldiers.

Let us ask Mary Immaculate for an unshakable faith and at least a drop of the infinite dignity of Jesus when the wicked, with their laughter, mock our faithfulness to the morality of Holy Church.

Our Father: God's ineffable beauty.

Hail Mary:
1. The third stripping of Jesus.
2. His crown of thorns.
3. The cloth with which He was blindfolded.
4. The blows and spit with which His face was covered.
5. The old cloak placed on His shoulders.
6. The reed that was stuck in His hand.
7. The sharp stone on which He was seated.
8. The outrages and insults hurled at Him.
9. The blood and sweat that issued from His adorable head.
10. The hairs pulled from His head and beard.

FOURTH SORROWFUL MYSTERY
The CARRYING of the CROSS

"They hated Me without cause."
John 15:25

In this mystery we contemplate our Divine Master—"the reproach of men and the Man of Sorrows"—bearing the crushing burden of the Cross, which tears His flesh and lays bare His bones.

By the shoulder wound of Christ, let us ask the Mother of Sorrows for the grace to proceed with supernatural determination in our spiritual lives and in our apostolate even when we fall under the weight of the cross.

Our Father: God's unlimited omnipotence.

Hail Mary:
1. Our Lord's presentation to the people with the "Ecce Homo."
2. Barabbas being preferred to Our Lord.
3. The false witnesses brought against Him.
4. His condemnation to death.
5. The love with which He embraced and kissed His Cross.
6. The frightful pains He had while carrying it.
7. His falls from sheer weakness under its weight.
8. The painful meeting with His Holy Mother.
9. Veronica's veil, marked with the imprint of His face.
10. His tears and those of His Holy Mother and the pious women who accompanied Him to Calvary.

FIFTH SORROWFUL MYSTERY
The CRUCIFIXION

"Father, into Thy Hands
I commend My Spirit."
Luke 23:46

In this mystery we contemplate our Divine Savior nailed to the Cross and raised aloft between two thieves. He is plunged in an ocean of bitterness; He is abandoned by the Father Himself.

Let us ask the Blessed Mother, who stands at the foot of the Cross, to grant us the grace of taking our vocation to its last consequences and of loving the sacrifices it entails.

Our Father: God's frightful justice.

Hail Mary:
1. The five wounds of Jesus and the blood He shed on the Cross.
2. His pierced heart and the Cross upon which He was crucified.
3. The nails and lance that pierced Him, and the sponge of vinegar and gall given Him to drink.
4. The shame and infamy He suffered being crucified naked between two thieves.
5. The compassion of His Holy Mother.
6. His seven last words.
7. His abandonment and silence.
8. The affliction of the whole universe.
9. His cruel and ignominious death.
10. His taking down from the Cross and His burial.

FIRST GLORIOUS MYSTERY
The RESURRECTION

"Bring hither thy hand, and put it into My Side; and be not faithless, but believing."
John 20:27

In this mystery we contemplate our Divine Redeemer rising through His own power on the third day. His body is in a state of glory: His wounds are now tokens of His triumph over death.

Let us ask Our Lady of Fatima for a staunch hope in the triumph of her Immaculate Heart and a jubilant enthusiasm in the anticipation of her kingdom.

Our Father: God's infinite eternity.

Hail Mary:
1. The descent of the soul of Our Lord into hell.
2. The joy of the souls of the holy fathers, and their departure from limbo.
3. The rejoining of His soul and body in the sepulcher.
4. His miraculous exit from the sepulcher.
5. His victories over death and sin, the world and the devil.
6. The four glorious qualities of His body.
7. The power in heaven and on earth that He received from His Father.
8. The apparitions with which He honored His Holy Mother, His Apostles and His disciples.
9. The conversations about heaven that He had with His Apostles, and the meal He partook with them.
10. The authority and mission He gave them to preach throughout the world.

SECOND GLORIOUS MYSTERY
The ASCENSION

*"And behold, I am with you all days, even
to the consummation of the world."*
Matthew 28:20

In this mystery we contemplate the Just One withdrawing from His disciples and ascending into heaven forty days after His resurrection: it is the concluding work of redemption.

By this final elevation of Our Lord's human nature into the condition of divine glory, let us ask the Most Holy Virgin for the ultimate exaltation of Holy Mother Church and Christian civilization.

Our Father: God's boundless immensity.

Hail Mary:
1. The promise Jesus made to His Apostles that He would send them the Holy Ghost, and the order He gave them to prepare themselves to receive Him.
2. The gathering of all His disciples on Mount Olivet.
3. The blessing He gave them as He ascended from this earth to heaven.
4. His glorious and admirable ascension, by His own power, into the empyrean heaven.
5. The reception and divine triumph given Him by God, His Father, and the whole celestial court.
6. The triumphant power with which He opened the gates of heaven, where no mortal had ever entered.
7. His sitting at the right hand of His Father as His well-beloved Son and equal.
8. The power He received to judge the living and the dead.
9. His second coming, in which His might and majesty will appear in all their splendor.
10. The justice He will do in the Last Judgment, rewarding the good and chastising the evil for all eternity.

THIRD GLORIOUS MYSTERY
The DESCENT *of the* HOLY GHOST

"And there appeared to them parted tongues as it were of fire, and it sat upon every one of them."
Acts 2:3

In this mystery we contemplate Our Lord fulfilling His words to the Apostles: "I will ask the Father, and He shall give you another Paraclete, that He may abide with you forever" (John 14:16). The Apostles, gathered around Our Lady in the Cenacle, are now so filled with the Holy Ghost that they seem drunk (Acts 2:13).

Let us ask the Spouse of the Holy Ghost to say but a word and thus transform our weak, lukewarm and sinful souls.

Our Father: God's universal providence.

Hail Mary:
1. The truth of the Holy Ghost, God Who proceeds from the Father and the Son, and Who is the Heart of the Divinity.
2. The sending of the Holy Ghost by the Father and the Son to the Apostles.
3. The great noise with which He descended, a sign of His strength and power.
4. The tongues of fire He placed upon the Apostles to give them knowledge of the Scriptures, and love of God and neighbor.
5. The plenitude of graces with which He distinguished Mary, His faithful spouse.
6. His marvellous control over all the saints and over the person of Jesus Christ Himself, Whom He guided during His whole life.
7. The twelve fruits of the Holy Ghost.
8. The seven gifts of the Holy Ghost.
9. To request particularly the gift of wisdom and the coming of His reign over the hearts of men.
10. To obtain victory over the evil spirits opposed to Him; namely, the spirits of the world, the flesh and the devil.

FOURTH GLORIOUS MYSTERY
The ASSUMPTION

*"Thou are the glory of Jerusalem,
thou art the joy of Israel, thou art
the honor of our people."*
Judith 15:10

In this mystery we contemplate the Virgin Mary being taken body and soul into heaven by God amidst the rejoicing of the angels.

Let us ask our celestial Mother to fill us with faith and to make us pure and strong, so that we may fight worthily for her on earth and rejoice with her in heaven forever.

Our Father: God's indescribable liberality.

Hail Mary:
1. The eternal predestination of Mary as the masterpiece of God's hands.
2. Her Immaculate Conception, and her plenitude of grace and reason while within the womb of her mother, Saint Anne.
3. Her nativity, which gladdened the whole universe.
4. Her presentation and stay in the Temple.
5. Her admirable life exempt from all sin.
6. The fullness of her singular virtues.
7. Her fertile virginity and painless birth.
8. Her divine maternity and her alliance with the Most Holy Trinity.
9. Her precious and loving death.
10. Her resurrection and triumphant assumption.

FIFTH GLORIOUS MYSTERY
The CORONATION

"For behold, from henceforth all generations shall call me blessed."

In this mystery we contemplate the Daughter of God, the Mother of God, the Spouse of God, addressed in the words of the Canticle of Canticles "Come: thou shalt be crowned," and made empress and mistress of all creation.

Let us ask our Queen that, from the height of glory on which she was placed, she will be for us a Mother of Mercy, raising us when we fall, loving us at every moment, so that, like the angels, we may faithfully serve her in all things.

Our Father: God's inaccessible glory.

Hail Mary:
1. The triple crown with which the Most Holy Trinity crowned Mary.
2. The joy and new glory heaven received by her triumph.
3. To recognize her as Queen of Heaven and Earth, angels and men.
4. The treasurer of the graces of God, of the merits of Jesus Christ and of the gifts of the Holy Ghost.
5. The mediatrix and advocate of men.
6. The destroyer and ruin of the devil and of heresies.
7. The secure refuge of sinners.
8. The mother and nurturer of Christians.
9. The joy and sweetness of the just.
10. The universal refuge of the living, the all-powerful consolation of the afflicted, of the dying and of the souls in Purgatory.

The FIVE FIRST SATURDAYS

On December 10, 1925, Our Lady promised Sister Lucia she would "...assist at the hour of death, with the graces necessary for salvation, all those who on the first Saturdays of five consecutive months confess, receive Holy Communion, pray a rosary, and keep me company for a quarter of an hour meditating on the fifteen mysteries with the intention of offering me reparation."

There are four requirements to faithfully fulfil the Five First Saturdays.

1. Go to confession.
2. Receive Holy Communion.
3. Say five decades of the Holy Rosary.
4. Meditate for a quarter of an hour on the fifteen mysteries of the rosary (separate from praying the rosary).

During an apparition on February 15, 1926, because of the difficulty that some people had to be able to confess on a Saturday, Sister Lucia asked Our Lord if the confession would be valid if done within a period of eight days before or eight days after the first Saturday. Our Lord answered: "Yes, it can even be within many more days, provided they are in the state of grace when they receive Me, and have the intention of offering reparation to the Immaculate Heart of Mary."

Our Lord explained to Sister Lucia why five first Saturdays—there are five kinds of offenses and blasphemies committed against the Immaculate Heart of Mary:

1. Those committed against the Immaculate Conception

2. Those committed against the virginity of Our Lady
3. Those committed against the Divine maternity, refusing at the same time, to accept her as the mother of men
4. Those committed by men who publicly attempt to instill indifference, scorn, and even hatred for this Immaculate Mother in the hearts of children
5. Those committed by men who insult her directly in her sacred images.

A BRIEF HISTORY
of the ROSARY

The word rosary means crown of roses. In pre-Christian times, pagans used to crown their statues with roses to symbolize the rendering of their hearts to the gods. With the coming of Christianity, the fusing of their love for false gods with their hatred for the early Christians led to the Roman persecutions.

During these persecutions, Christian virgins, dressed in their best and crowned with roses, went to their martyrdom in the sandy arena of the Coliseum. Their brethren in the Faith later collected these crowns of roses and prayed before them, saying one prayer per rose.

Among these prayers, that which held the foremost place in Christian hearts from the beginning was the one that flowed from the lips of our Divine Redeemer Himself: the Our Father.

Little by little, as though to complement this most perfect prayer, the Holy Ghost inspired the faithful to address the Mother of the Redeemer with the words spoken by the angel and by Saint Elizabeth, giving rise to the recitation of the first part of the Hail Mary.

The Church added the name of Mary to the beginning and that of Jesus to the end of this salutation.

At the Council of Ephesus, in 431, Holy Mother Church defined that the Blessed Virgin is truly the Mother of God and gave us the conclusion of the Hail Mary: "Holy Mary, Mother of God...," which officially became the second part of the Hail Mary in 1568.

In the monasteries of the Middle Ages, the monks who could not read replaced the recitation of the Psalms with the repetition of the Our Father. Since there are 150 Psalms in the Bible, they prayed a series of 150 Our Fathers, which they called the "Psalter of Christ." To count the Our Fathers, the monks used knotted ropes or collars of grains, which in France came to be called "patenôtres."

In the eleventh century, some hermits and laymen began to recite "Our Lady's Psalter," that is, 150 salutations "Hail Mary. . . fruit of thy womb," instead of the 150 Our Fathers. They divided these salutations into three series of 50, which they termed "rosaries" or "crowns" because of the custom of crowning Our Lady's statues with flowers.

But it was only in 1214, according to a pious and admirable tradition, that the Most Holy Virgin herself consecrated this devotion by appearing to Saint Dominic of Guzman, founder of the Dominicans, and giving him the rosary in its present form as a weapon to combat the Albigensian heresy that was devastating southern France.

Let the great apostle of Mary, Saint Louis de Montfort, tell us the circumstances in which that great event took place:

"Saint Dominic, seeing that the gravity of people's sins was hindering the conversion of the Albigensians, withdrew into a forest near Toulouse where he prayed unceasingly for three days and three nights. During this time he did nothing but weep and do harsh penances in order to appease the anger of Almighty God. He used his discipline so much that his body was lacerated, and finally he fell into a coma.

"At this point Our Lady appeared to him, accompanied by three angels, and she said:

"'Dear Dominic, do you know which weapon the Blessed Trinity wants to use to reform the world?'

"'Oh, my Lady,' answered Saint Dominic, 'you know far better than I do because, next to your Son Jesus Christ, you have always been the chief instrument of our salvation.'

"Then Our Lady replied:

"'I want you to know that, in this kind of warfare, the battering ram has always been the Angelic Psalter which is the foundation stone of the New Testament. Therefore, if you want to reach these hardened souls and win them over to God, preach my Psalter.'

"So he arose, comforted, and burning with zeal for the conversion of the people in that district he made straight for the Cathedral. At once, unseen angels rang the bells to gather the people together and Saint Dominic began to preach.

"At the very beginning of his sermon an appalling storm broke out, the earth shook, the sun was darkened, and there was so much thunder and lightning that all were very much afraid. Even greater was their fear when, looking at a picture of Our Lady exposed in a prominent place, they saw her raise her arms to heaven three times to call down God's vengeance upon them if they failed to be converted, to amend their lives, and seek the protection of the Holy Mother of God.

"At last, at the prayer of Saint Dominic, the storm

came to an end, and he went on preaching. So fervently and compellingly did he explain the importance and value of the Holy rosary that almost all the people of Toulouse embraced it and renounced their false beliefs" (*The Secret of the Rosary*, Montfort Publications, Bay Shore, N.Y., 1954, pp. 18-19).

After this brilliant victory of the Faith, obtained by preaching the rosary, Saint Dominic endeavoured, with renewed fervor to spread this meritorious devotion. But after his death in 1221, as the memory of his preaching gradually faded in the minds of the Christians who had heard him, devotion to the rosary declined.

One century later it was practically buried and forgotten.

To re-establish this devotion in its pristine fervour, Our Lady chose Blessed Alan de la Roche, a Dominican from the monastery at Dinan, France. In 1464, after apparitions of Our Lord, Our Lady and Saint Dominic himself, Blessed Alan solemnly resolved to preach the rosary incessantly, which he did until his death in 1475, around the time of the founding of the Confraternity of the Holy Rosary at the Dominican convent at Cologne. It was to him and Saint Dominic that Our Lady gave her promises to those who pray the rosary. (These promises appear on page 47 of this book.)

The erection of confraternities in many other places led to the printing of numerous books on the rosary. The devotion quickly spread throughout Europe. It is to the confraternities that the acceptance of the list of fifteen mysteries to be meditated on during the recitation of the Hail Mary's is mainly due. Pope Saint Pius V, a Dominican himself, enunciated the list in his *Consueverunt* of 1569.

By then, Europe was tragically menaced by the

might of the Turkish Empire. Saint Pius V convoked a crusade to save Christendom. However, many Christian peoples, either rendered lukewarm by the Renaissance or alienated from the bosom of the Church by Protestantism, turned a deaf ear to the Pope. But the Holy Father did not rest until he had organized a fleet of about 200 galleys from the Papal States, Malta, Spain, Naples and Sicily, and the states of Venice and Genoa.

This Christian fleet, placed under the Most Holy Virgin's protection by the Pope, sailed under the command of Don Juan of Austria, half-brother of King Philip II of Spain. The Muslim fleet was sighted about 50 miles west of the harbor of Lepanto, which is just inside the narrow entrance of the Gulf of Corinth.

Battle was joined on October 7, 1571. Upon its outcome depended the future of Christendom.

During four long hours, galleys crashed into each other, musket balls and arrows flew everywhere, men swarmed aboard the enemy ships wherever they could get a grip.

Although things had gone badly for the Christians at first, in the end they were victorious. Ali Pasha, the commander-in-chief of the Muslim fleet, was killed and his standard taken. The Muslims, losing courage, began to flee.

The combat became a slaughter of infidels. It is reckoned that 24,000 Muslims were killed and 5,000 taken prisoner. The Christians captured 177 ships and freed perhaps as many as 15,000 Christian rowers, slaves in the Turkish galleys.

On the day of the battle, Saint Pius V was working with the cardinals. Suddenly, interrupting his work and opening the window, he looked at the sky and cried out: "A truce to business; our great task at present is to thank God for the victory He has just given the Christian army."

More than two weeks later, a courier, delayed by storms at sea, arrived in Rome with the news of the naval victory of Lepanto. The Pope wept for joy: the power of Islam had been dealt a shattering blow from which it will hopefully never recover. To thank the Most Holy Virgin for this triumph obtained while the members of all the confraternities of Rome were holding rosary processions, Saint Pius V added to the Litany of the Blessed Virgin Mary the supplication "Help of Christians" and instituted for the first Sunday of October the feast of Our Lady of Victory, which was changed by Gregory XIII to the feast of the Most Holy Rosary.

After a new victory over the Turks gained by Prince Eugene of Savoy in 1716, at the Battle of Peterwardein in Hungary, Pope Clement XI extended the celebration of the feast of the rosary to the universal Church. The great Saint Pius X fixed the feast on October 7.

In 1917, less than three years after the death of Saint Pius X, Our Lady appeared to three shepherd children, Lucia, Francisco and Jacinta (aged ten, nine and seven respectively), at Cova da Iria, Fatima, Portugal, in a series of six apparitions that began May 13 and ended October 13. The authenticity of these apparitions was confirmed by the miracle of the sun witnessed by about 70,000 spectators during the final apparition.

At Fatima, Our Lady gave the three children the mission of telling the world that she was profoundly displeased with the impiety and corruption of men. She warned that if mankind did not amend its ways a terrible chastisement would come, several nations would be annihilated, Russia would spread its errors throughout the world and the Holy Father would have much to suffer.

In her message, the Queen of Heaven and Earth, along with pointing out the danger, tells us how to avoid it. She maternally provides guidelines to avert this terrible chastisement: she asks for prayer and penance, and especially the recitation of the Holy Rosary.

It was after giving the warning of the chastisement and the ways to avoid it that Our Lady taught us the prayer to be recited at the end of each mystery of the rosary. She told Lucia: "When you pray the rosary, after each decade say, 'O my Jesus, forgive us our sins, save us from the fires of hell; lead all souls to heaven, especially those in most need of Thy mercy.'"

At the tempestuous beginning of the twenty-first century, amidst the most devastating crisis in history, a beacon of hope shines in the words spoken by Our Lady at Fatima, for she has assured us: "Finally, my Immaculate Heart will triumph!"

The FIFTEEN PROMISES of MARY MOST HOLY
to Those Who Pray the Rosary

1. Whoever shall faithfully serve me by the recitation of the rosary shall receive signal graces.
2. I promise my special protection and the greatest graces to all those who shall recite the rosary.
3. The rosary shall be a powerful armor against hell; it will destroy vice, decrease sin and defeat heresy.
4. It will cause virtue and good works to flourish; it will obtain for souls the abundant mercy of God; it will withdraw the hearts of men from the love of the world and its vanities, and will

lift them to the desire of eternal things. Oh, that souls would sanctify themselves by this means!

5. The soul that recommends itself to me by the recitation of the rosary shall not perish.

6. Whoever shall recite the rosary devoutly, applying himself to the consideration of its sacred mysteries, shall never be conquered by misfortune: if he be a sinner, he shall not perish by an unprovided death; if he be just, he shall remain in the grace of God. He shall become worthy of eternal life.

7. Whoever shall have a true devotion for the rosary shall not die without the sacraments of the Church.

8. Those who are faithful to the recitation of the rosary shall have, during their life and at their death the light of God and the plenitude of His graces. At the moment of death they shall participate in the merits of the saints in paradise.

9. I shall deliver from purgatory those who have been devoted to the rosary.

10. The faithful children of the rosary shall merit a high degree of glory in heaven.

11. You shall obtain all you ask of me by the recitation of the rosary.

12. All those who propagate the Holy Rosary shall be aided by me in their necessities.

13. I have obtained from my Divine Son that all the advocates of the rosary shall have for intercessors the entire celestial court during their life and at the hour of death.

14. All who recite the rosary are my sons, and brothers of my son, Jesus Christ.

15. Devotion to my rosary is a great sign of predestination.